The Unforgettable Boxcar

The Untold True Story of Friendship, Hawaiian Tradition, and a Heroic Little Boxcar

Janet Lorimer & Kerry Lorimer

Visit us on online at www.theunforgettableboxcar.com

This book presents a historical account of the 1947 Friendship Train, the 1949 Merci Train and Boxcars, and the restoration efforts done by the Hawaiian Railway Society, and while the authors have strived to provide the most accurate representation possible, it is important to recognize that historical interpretations can vary.

Edited by Ellen Wettersten

Book design by Claudia Gadotti
Illustrations by Claudia Gadotti

Identifiers: ISBN 9798999071101 (trade) | ISBN 9798999071118 (ebook)
ISBN 9798999071125 (hardcover)

Library of Congress Control Number: 2025918366
Green Valley

First edition 2025

This labor of love is dedicated to the millions
of ordinary people who come together to give
from their hearts in big ways and small.
You inspire the world.

"`A`ohe hana nui ke alu like'ia. No task is too great when done together by all."

-Hawaiian Proverb

Chapter 1

The little French boxcar stood in the middle of a hot, dusty train yard in Hawai`i, far apart from the other train cars and locomotives.

There were five big locomotives. Three were yellow, one was green, and one was the color of candied apples. There was also a very special parlor car because Queen Lili`uokalani, the last beloved monarch of the Kingdom of Hawai`i, had ridden in it.

There were other boxcars as well, big American boxcars, painted in protective coats of brick red.

People loved the beautiful train cars. They took pictures of them and gathered around as the storyteller placed a hand on a railcar or engine and told stories of days gone by.

But everyone ignored the little boxcar. It had an amazing

story, too, but no one seemed to care because the story had been forgotten.

The little boxcar didn't look like anything special. The sun, rain, termites, and years of neglect had done a lot of damage. Its paint was cracked and faded. Its metal was rusting. There were holes in the sides, and much of the roof and floor were gone.

Sometimes people glanced at the boxcar. Then they'd walk away. No one knew that the boxcar had done amazing things most boxcars don't do. No one knew that it had crossed two oceans to bring a wonderful gift to the people of Hawai`i.

No one knew that, a long time ago, the little French boxcar had been a hero.

Chapter 2

The little boxcar was built in France in the late 1800s. It didn't have a name, just the letter *J* and five numbers painted on the door. It was an ordinary boxcar, but people relied on it. Workers loaded food, paper products, tools, and cloth into the boxcar. Then they put their hands on the door, grasped the handle, and pulled it shut. With a hiss of steam and shrill blasts from the locomotive's whistle, the little boxcar traveled across France, its wheels clickity-clacking against the rails as it delivered things people needed every day.

France had been friends with America since the American Revolution. Then in 1914, a war broke out in Europe. At the time, it was called the Great War because so many countries fought in it. Today it is commonly referred to as World War I. Many of the battles were fought in France, so to help win the war, American soldiers went to France and fought alongside French soldiers.

During the war, the boxcar's job changed. Sometimes it carried soldiers into battle and to safety, speeding down the track to avoid being hit by explosives. Other times, it brought horses for the soldiers to use. The boxcar could carry either 40 *Hommes* or 8 *Chevaux*, meaning it could carry either 40 soldiers or 8 horses. By law, that had to be painted on the outside of the boxcars, so the American soldiers called those boxcars "forty-and-eights."

Riding in the boxcar was hot and crowded. The soldiers sat on hard, wooden benches, swaying back and forth as the boxcar rode on the rails. But they appreciated the boxcar. It saved them from walking many miles and getting sore feet or wearing out their boots. And when they heard the "rat-tat-tat" of guns in the distance, they were grateful they weren't fighting in the trenches.

One of those soldiers was John Rowe from Hawai`i. John was descended on his mother's side from King Kamehameha the Great. He fought alongside his brothers-in-arms, the 39th Infantry Regiment, during the Aisne-Marne Operation, a major battle fought in France in July 1918. Although he had the blood of warriors and kings in him, he was killed in action in that battle and buried in the land of his ancestors at O`ahu Cemetery.

The war ended on November 11, 1918, and the boxcar carried the surviving soldiers to safety one last time.

As they climbed out of the boxcar, they put their hands on the wood and remembered those who would not be going home. Two years later, members of the veterans' organization, The American Legion, formed a special group to help children. They called their group *La Société des Quarante Hommes et Huit Chevaux* (The Society of Forty Men and Eight Horses) in honor of what the 40 *et* 8 boxcars meant to them.

The little boxcar made it through the Great War without getting damaged and went back to work delivering things people needed. But now some things were harder to get. Cities and villages had been destroyed, trenches and craters scarred the land, and chemical weapons had poisoned the earth. Millions of people had died. Unexploded ordnance (UXO) explosives that did not detonate in the war are still being found today.

Everyone hoped that would be the last war ever fought.

After the war, PLM, the company that owned the boxcar, gave the little boxcar a new name: K-128220. They engraved the name on a metal plate and fastened it to the frame. The *K* and the numbers told people that the little boxcar had a lever brake, which was similar to a parking brake on a car. However, PLM wanted modern train cars that were safer and more efficient, so they built new boxcars that had air brakes instead of lever brakes.

PLM continued to use some of the older boxcars, at least for a little while. K-128220 couldn't do the same things it used to do, but it kept working in a limited fashion.

Chapter 3

In 1939, another war broke out. It was called World War II because so many countries fought in it. France surrendered to Germany one year later, and the Nazis controlled France for four years. They forced the French to live by their rules. They seized homes, schools, businesses, and train stations. They told people where they could and could not go, and they told people what they could and could not eat. They stole art from museums. Food and fuel were hard to come by. Worst of all, the Nazis took people away by force from their homes and families. Many were never seen again.

People were cold and hungry and very, very scared.

No one in the United States wanted to be part of another war. Many were still recovering from the First World War. But on December 7, 1941, the people living in Hawai`i awoke to a horrible sound.

Whoo-BOOM!

Fearing for their lives, people scrambled as waves of fighter planes from the Empire of Japan dropped bombs on the U.S. naval base at Pu`uloa, also known as Pearl Harbor. The sky was black with smoke, and over the wail of sirens, the "rat-tat-tat-tat" of guns could be heard as American servicemen fought back. When the attack was over, battleships had sunk, planes were destroyed, buildings were ablaze, and more than two thousand military and civilian Americans had died.

Martial law was declared in Hawai`i, giving the military full authority over civilian rights. Once again, American servicemen went overseas to fight for freedom, and the Territory of Hawai`i sent some of her best men. Despite hostilities that Americans of Japanese ancestry faced, thousands of nisei, or "second generation" Americans of Japanese ancestry, were loyal to America and answered the call to serve. Their parents were Japanese immigrants, or issei (first generation). On June 4, 1942, over 1,400 members of the Hawai`i National Guard were shipped out in secrecy, without saying good-bye to their families or loved ones. They became the 100th Infantry Battalion, known as the "one *Puka Puka*" (*puka* means "hole"), a then primarily nisei battalion whose motto was "Remember Pearl Harbor." Over two thousand more Hawai`i nisei enlisted, and with the 100th, became the 442nd Regimental Combat Team (RCT), a segregated combat unit. To this day, the 442nd RCT is considered the most decorated unit for its size and length of service in U.S. military history.

World War II lasted six long years. During that time, soldiers again rode to battle and to safety in boxcars, placing their hands on the door as they climbed on and off. Like soldiers in the Great War, they also appreciated the 40 & 8s. And when the war ended, they talked about what it was like to ride in boxcars with 40 *Hommes*, 8 *Chevaux* painted on the doors.

But mostly, they remembered those who would not go home.

The little boxcar worked as long as it could, until one day someone decided it was too old. K-128220 was taken to a train yard and left there. Days passed, then months. The rain fell and the sun beat down on the little boxcar's roof. Its paint cracked and weeds grew up around its wheels.

No one came to see it. The boxcar that was useful to people who needed things and useful to people who'd served in wartime had been forgotten.

Everyone wanted to return to a normal life, but after two world wars, it was very hard. Millions more had died or were homeless. Factories were destroyed. And the winter was so cold and the summer so hot that the crops died before they could be harvested. People in Europe were starving, and although governments tried to help, it wasn't enough.

Chapter 4

An American journalist named Drew Pearson believed that average Americans could do a better job helping their European friends than governments. In October 1947, he came up with a plan to collect enough food to fill a mile-long train. The train would begin its journey in California before traveling across the country with eight boxcars. At each stop, people would give what they could. The boxcars would be unloaded in New York and the supplies shipped to France. He called his mile-long train the *Friendship Train*.

To see if anyone liked his idea, he wrote about it in his newspaper column and talked about it on the radio. He called it "a genuine sacrifice from the heart of America." Other newspapers around the country were inspired to print articles about the *Friendship Train*.

The spirit of the *Friendship Train* quickly grew. Americans loved the idea and wanted the food to arrive in France by Christmas.

Ordinary people like teachers, farmers, and truck drivers all volunteered to help. Children collected pennies, nickels, and dimes, as well as canned and dried foods. They donated their ice cream money to buy wheat. Groups like the Boy Scouts, Girl

Scouts, and Campfire Girls raised money, too. Across the country students from elementary schools to colleges all found ways to give to the *Friendship Train*.

Drew Pearson wanted the train to travel from California to New York, making many stops along the way so more boxcars could be added. But people in other states wanted to help, too. So, on their own, they filled other boxcars and connected them to locomotives traveling to New York to meet Drew Pearson's train. As a result, many friendship trains were created.

Locomotives steamed into train stations throughout America as crowds cheered upon hearing the iconic CHUFF-chuff -chuff -chuff, CHUFF-chuff-chuff-chuff, WHOO-WOO.

There were ceremonies and parades with bands playing, flags waving, and people singing patriotic songs. A film crew traveling on board Drew Pearson's *Friendship Train* captured images of people celebrating at every station. And as volunteers loaded the donations on board, people wrote kind messages on the boxcars and patted the train in a gesture of goodwill for friends they'd never met across the Atlantic.

Chapter 5

Meanwhile, in 1947, the people of Hawai`i were also trying to rebuild their lives. It was not easy. Many serious things had happened in the islands that most people on the mainland did not know about.

The Kingdom of Hawai`i was overthrown by foreign businessmen in 1893, just fifty-four years earlier. The Kānaka Maoli (native Hawaiians) were devastated when their flag was lowered and replaced with the flag of another country. Hawai`i's public education system is the only one established by a monarch, King Kamehameha III. But in 1896, an English-only law was passed banning 'Ōlelo Hawai`i (Hawaiian language) from being taught in public schools. People were angry when the *`āina* (land) and their homes were taken from them. They were told where they could and could not live. The jobs they were given paid poorly.

Some of the `āina became sugar plantations. People from Japan, China, Korea, Portugal, Puerto Rico, and the Philippines came to work on the plantations because they wanted a better life. But the work was hard, they were treated badly, and wages were low. They were paid differently based on where they came from and the color of their skin.

More than a third of Hawai`i's residents in 1941 were of Japanese ancestry. After the attack on Pu`uloa (Pearl Harbor), people everywhere were angry and afraid. The U.S. government at that time called people of Japanese ancestry "enemy aliens" even if they were Americans. When martial law was declared, people who had done nothing wrong were arrested and kept in cells or in camps with barbed wire fences and armed guards until the war ended. This also included people of Italian ancestry, as well as people of Irish and Scandinavian ancestry, who were arrested and held as Germans. The camp was located about thirteen miles from Pu`uloa and less than seven miles away from two sugar mills.

ANNEXATION
"HERE TO STAY!"
And the star-spangled banner
In triumph shall wave,
O'er the Isles of Hawaii
And the homes of the brave

Most of the sugar plantations were owned by a select few. They controlled their employees' lives by keeping people apart based on where they came from. Finally, tired of the poor housing, long hours, low pay, and years of disrespect, the plantation workers banded together and went on strike in 1946. It was a very difficult decision. Without work, they risked losing what little they had. It was tempting to give up. But the plantation workers unified and supported each other. After almost three challenging months, the strike was over and new laws were passed to help them.

Chapter 6

Hawai`i was not a state in 1947. And no effort was made by Drew Pearson or his associates to include the territory in the *Friendship Train* campaign. But when Americans were asked to help a starving nation in whatever way they could, the historical events of Hawai`i did not stop the people in the land of *aloha* (love) from wanting to aid their friends overseas on their own.

Hawaiian culture teaches a very important concept called *kokua,* which dates all the way back to ancient times. It means choosing to help others without expecting anything in return. *Kokua* is a way to live life based on kindness and respect. The *akamai* (smart)

Hawaiians knew that if people came together in *laulima* (cooperation), the whole community would be strong, regardless of whether they were *Kānaka Maoli* (native Hawaiian), *kama`āina* (a local resident regardless of race) or *malihini* (a visitor to the islands).

Thanks to the *Friendship Train,* people on the mainland were practicing kokua. They just didn't know it.

Hawai`i had something that was badly needed in France: sugar. But the Hawaiian Islands are over two thousand miles from the mainland. And the *Friendship Train* was scheduled to leave Los Angeles within a week. How would they get a boxcar full of sugar to California?

In fact, the sugar was already in California. After the sugar cane was harvested, it was taken to a sugar mill where juice from the sugar cane was turned into raw sugar. It looked like brown crystals.

Then the raw sugar was sold to a refinery in California. The refinery turned the raw sugar into white sugar. All the people in Hawai`i had to do was raise enough money to buy the sugar from the refinery. Then the sugar could be loaded into a boxcar in California.

The Hawaiian sugar industry offered to pay for the sugar, but the people said no. They wanted to pay for it themselves. A pound of sugar cost eight and a quarter cents in 1947. Hawai`i had five days to raise the $6,500 needed to buy enough sugar to fill one boxcar. That would be

almost $90,000 today.

People on O'ahu as well as those on the outer islands like Molokai and the Island of Hawai`i, also known as the Big Island, immediately got involved. On Saturday, November 1, the *Honolulu Star-Bulletin* reported that three thousand "Friendship Cans" were distributed throughout the territory in stores, banks, factories, offices, lumberyards, hotels, and schools. With very little time until the deadline, employees and business owners, issei and nisei, military and civilian, students and teachers, union members, contractors, *Kānaka Maoli, kama`āina,* and *malihini* began dropping nickels and dimes into the cans as fast as they could. Groups like We the Women, the Veterans of Foreign Wars, and the Honolulu Chapter of the NAACP (National Association for the Advancement of Colored People) organized and spearheaded fundraising campaigns on a grand scale. And *keiki* (children) went door to door asking their neighbors to kokua for those overseas.

The people of Hawai`i raised $5,000 of the $6,500 needed in just two days. Inspired by this amazing achievement, they expanded their efforts. Donations poured in at Iolani Palace. Hawaiian Airlines employees collected donations on flights. And the University of Hawai`i proudly presented their gift in the form of a money lei. But while large groups, institutions, and corporations were able to raise a significant amount of money, the *Honolulu Star-Bulletin* reported that "most of the contributions came from the average man in the street."

At the end of the week, the Hawaiian Sugar Planters' Association added their donation to the total amount. By working together and with an average donation of eight cents, the people of Hawai`i raised $13,000 in seven days, twice as much as they needed. Hawai`i sent not one but two boxcars full of sugar to Europe.

In an article covering the Friendship Train sendoff ceremony in Los Angeles, the Honolulu Star-Bulletin wrote "Hawai`i stole the show from Hollywood tonight." The Governor of Hawai`i gave a speech at the ceremony in which he said that the carloads of sugar represented nickels and dimes contributed by workers on the plantation, schoolchildren and men and women from every walk of life.

Before the boxcars were hooked up to the *Friendship Train* someone painted "Sugar from the people of Hawai`i" on the outside. They were the first and second boxcars on the *Friendship Train*.

Chapter 7

The *Friendship Train* left Los Angeles on November 7, 1947, and began its journey across the country. It was decorated with banners, slogans of goodwill, and *Vive La France* (Long Live France) painted on the outside. America had forty-eight days until the Christmas deadline. The *Friendship Train* reached New York on November 18 with 225 boxcars attached. More trains steamed into stations in the Big Apple with 270 boxcars filled with goods. Another 100 boxcars arrived, sent by other groups wanting to help, and New York gave enough cargo to fill over 25 boxcars.

Drew Pearson's mile-long train was much, much longer.

That same day, 25,000 people crowded New York's City Hall to hear speeches, three of which were given by American children in English, French, and Italian. Then, as people listened, they heard another child's voice coming over the crackling sound of a shortwave radio. Broadcasting from France, the child thanked America for its generosity.

FRIENDSHIP CARGO
UNITED STATES LINES

Americans had donated food that could be stored for a long time without spoiling, like wheat and rice and flour. They gave powdered eggs and powdered milk...dried peas, beans, and dried fruit...canned meat and pasta...baby food...and lots and lots of sugar. In addition, the money collected was used to buy even more food to make sure no one would go hungry.

They also sent clothing to keep people warm, coal to heat their homes, soap, vitamins, and medical supplies. They included personalized notes of friendship and goodwill. America had gone above and beyond what Drew Pearson had hoped for

At New York Harbor, the supplies were unloaded from all the boxcars and loaded into the hold of a huge cargo ship. However, there was a problem. There was more cargo than one ship could hold. Three more ships were added to transport the remaining goods to Europe.

The first ship was given a new name. It was now called the *Friend Ship*. Someone painted "Friendship Cargo United States Lines" and "Gifts of Food from U.S.A. to France" in big white letters on the dark hull for everyone to see. On December 7, 1947, six years after America entered World War II, the *Friend Ship* left for France with over 3,000 tons of food and supplies.

Chapter 8

The *Friend Ship* docked in a harbor at the French city of Le Havre eight days before Christmas. Hawai`i's sugar had crossed the Pacific Ocean, the United States, and the Atlantic Ocean before reaching France. Their sweet gift of aloha traveled farther than anyone else's.

The supplies were unloaded and put on trucks. Six days before Christmas, fifty French army trucks loaded with food drove

through Paris. The trucks were greeted by school children with welcoming smiles. They were waving French flags and cheering.

Some of the supplies were put on another train called the *Train de l'Amitié (Friendship Train)*. The French *Friendship Train* traveled from Paris to Marseille on Christmas Eve. What had begun as an idea of one man wanting to help became the reality for many as food was delivered into the hands of French citizens to be enjoyed on Christmas Day.

When the other ships arrived, the *Train de l'Amitié* was filled with more food and supplies to be delivered to other countries, including Italy, Greece, Germany, Norway, Belgium, Austria, and the Netherlands.

Finally, on May 27, 1948, the *Friendship Train's* inspirational journey came to an end.

But it was the beginning of a new adventure for the little French boxcar.

Chapter 9

The people of France were very grateful to the Americans and wanted to say *merci* (thank you). But how could post-war France thank an entire country for food, freedom, and friendship?

Two Frenchmen named André Picard and Louis Cast had a grand idea. They wanted to create a train like the American *Friendship Train,* but instead of using modern train cars, they wanted to send original 40 & 8 boxcars to America filled with very special merci gifts from their fellow citizens.

Cast and Picard were war veterans and railroad workers. They were very *akamai* (smart). They knew those boxcars were the perfect way to honor the blood shed by Americans in two world wars and the bond shared between two nations. They envisioned the 40 & 8 boxcars full of beautiful things from ordinary people with grateful hearts. Although France was still recovering, the French loved their country and wanted to share what they were proud of, a way of celebrating French culture with their American friends.

Picard and Cast decided each of the forty-eight American states would receive a boxcar. But since Hawai`i gave the gift of sugar and Washington, D.C. gave the gift of flour, an extra boxcar was added to be shared between the territory and the district.

There was just one problem: the original 40 & 8s were all but forgotten.

The hunt for forty-nine antique boxcars began. People combed through dusty train stations and rail yards, looking at shabby, broken boxcars.

One day, someone found K-128220. The neglected little boxcar was in bad shape. It was worn and run down. The sun, wind, and rain had done a lot of damage. It didn't look like anything special. But Picard and Cast knew that K-128220 and the other boxcars were special in a way that veterans would understand. The old boxcars had to be restored.

First K-128220 was cleaned and repaired to prepare it for its trip across the sea. Then it was given a fresh coat of dark gray paint to make it look new again. It was also given a new name, in honor of its service during World War I: J-58220, which was painted on the door.

While the repair work was being done, others were deciding how to transform ordinary boxcars into monuments. A famous French artist specializing in heraldry was chosen for the job. Heraldic symbols, such as coats-of-arms, had been used by European royalty for centuries. The artist created forty wooden shields for

each boxcar, calling them *Symboles de France* (Symbols of France) because each one had an image to represent the former French provinces.

He also created two more, one bearing an eagle similar to the American Great Seal and the other a steam engine with a red poppy, a white daisy, and a blue cornflower. The flowers represented the battlefields where servicemen had lost their lives.

Two of the boxcars were unveiled during a Paris ceremony in October 1948. They had been transformed into works of art and symbols of friendship, military sacrifice, and national pride. Two red, white, and blue banners—the colors of the French and American flags—were the final touch adorning each side of the boxcars along with the name of the new train.

One side read: *Train de la Reconnaissance Francaise*. The other: *Gratitude Train*.

Chapter 10

The spirit of the *Gratitude Train* spread throughout the country. After the horrors of war, France was ready to shine again.

Ordinary people from all across the country gave from their hearts. Some used their skills by knitting, crocheting, and sewing beautiful things. Designers in Lyon made forty-nine wedding dresses for American brides. A grandmother lovingly embroidered a satin christening cap with silk yarn for an American baby. A woman made lace by hand to thank the American Red Cross for their help during her husband's captivity.

In schools and homes, children drew pictures and made scrapbooks for their American "little brothers" and "little sisters." Artists made paintings and sculptures. The president of France gifted forty-nine Sévres vases (Sévres is a city known for its fine porcelain) while the Musée du Louvre (Museum of the Louvre), which had hidden valuable art from Nazi theft, donated a sketch.

People gave things they cherished, like church bells, stained glass, and rosaries. War orphans donated their toys. Those all too familiar with the sacrifices made by veterans and their families honored Americans with military medals. And a plumber contributed a copper teakettle and a note: "Thanks to America for being delivered from the Germans who had made me a prisoner at Dachau where American troops let me free on May the 1st, 1945."

Some gave their last treasure, such as a chipped candy dish

TRAIN DE LA
FRANÇAISE

that had survived a bombing raid in which more than four hundred homes were destroyed. The owner included a note apologizing for the dish's imperfection. A toy table came from a child, with a note that read, "In thanking you for the things you have sent us, we are sending you these gifts that we hope you will like. We would have liked to get to know you as well as your beautiful country." And the City of Saint-Dié-des-Vosges, where the newly discovered America was given its name in 1507, sent forty-nine documents honoring the historic event.

One account told of a woman who had lost everything but still wanted to give. She pressed her hand against a 40 & 8, its paint not yet dry, in a simple gesture of love to friends she'd never met across the Atlantic.

From mementos of the First World War and dolls wearing traditional dress to a king's carriage and an original motorcycle, people of all ages, from the city to the countryside, left family heirlooms, sentimental tokens, historical artifacts, and letters of gratitude at train stations throughout France.

The gifts were loaded into the little boxcars until all forty-nine were full. However, more kept pouring in, too many for the boxcars to carry. Thousands had to be left behind.

Nine-year-old Michèle Rennou sent the train off on the last leg of its journey on January 6, 1949, by waving a red railroader's flag in a ceremony at Montparnasse Station in Paris.

The *Train de la Reconnaissance Francaise* finally arrived at the Port of Le Havre carrying 250 tons of gifts, goodwill from a grateful nation, and a French language book about an elephant king named Babar.

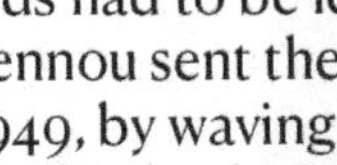

Chapter 11

The huge ship delivering the boxcars to America was called the *Magellan*, but for this journey, its name was changed to the *Gratitude Ship*. The words "Merci America" were painted on the freighter's dark hull, in white letters, ten feet tall, for everyone to see.

One by one, the boxcars full of gifts were lifted off their tracks and loaded onto the ship, where they were stored below the main deck and fastened together so they couldn't move. Then the *Gratitude Ship* set sail across the Atlantic Ocean on January 14, 1949.

It arrived in New York on February 1, 1949. Fleets of smaller boats welcomed the ship carrying the "Merci Boxcars" by sounding their horns and whistles in greeting as it sailed past the Statue of Liberty. Helicopters and jets flew overhead, and fireboat cannons shot into the sky columns of water that turned into pieces of ice in the winter air.

New York's "Merci Boxcar" was unloaded and put on a truck, where it was paraded up Broadway, with marching bands, showers of confetti, and 200,000 people cheering: "You're welcome!"

The 40 & 8 boxcars were not built the same as American train cars. They were smaller and had different brakes and operating systems, so they couldn't be hooked up to American locomotives. For the journey to their new homes, they were put on railroad flat cars. They may not have been on the rails, but they were part of a train one last time.

The states celebrated the arrival of their "Merci Boxcars" with ceremonies and speeches and stories about the war. People took pictures of the beautiful boxcars and admired the gifts, and they read the heartfelt letters from their friends overseas.

As the other boxcars were welcomed into their new homes, the forty-ninth boxcar that was meant to be shared still had a long way to go before it reached Hawai`i. First, it was taken to a rail yard in Washington, D.C., where some of the gifts were unloaded and the shields were removed. Then the flat car it was traveling on was hooked up to a train going west. When it reached California, a crane lifted the boxcar onto the *President Monroe*, a former navy vessel.

Once again at sea, J-58220 bobbed up and down with the ship on the waves of the Pacific Ocean. Like the gift of sugar, France's sweet thank-you gift to Hawai`i traveled farther than the others.

Chapter 12

The little boxcar arrived in Honolulu Harbor on November 9, 1949. The *President Monroe* used its big crane to lower J-58220 to the pier.

It was put on a trailer and taken to the American Legion post on McCully Street, where it was parked on a small, special rail made for a small, special boxcar. There was a ceremony to welcome J-58220 to its new home as people admired their "Merci" boxcar from France.

Some of the gifts were used as special prizes for children later on. The first two babies, a boy and a girl, born on Easter morning at Kapiolani Maternity Hospital received baby clothes lovingly donated to the *Gratitude Train* by a French mother. And a Farrington High School Junior was awarded a bracelet from the "Merci" boxcar for winning territorial first place in a National French contest.

But after that, people forgot about the boxcar. They forgot about the *Friendship Train*, the *Gratitude Train*, and the millions of ordinary people from two nations who came together to give from their hearts to those they'd never met.

More than thirty years passed. The rain fell and the sun beat down on the neglected boxcar's roof. Its wood warped and cracked. Its metal parts rusted. Its paint peeled and faded until the words 40 *Hommes*, 8 *Chevaux* vanished. People passed it every day, some in cars and some on foot. If they noticed it, they didn't realize how special it was.

Then, in the 1980s, J-58220 was moved again. McCully Street was going to be widened and there was no room in a growing city for an old relic.

At first, no one knew what to do with it. Finally, it was put on a truck and taken to `Ewa, a small town surrounded by miles of

PRESIDENT MONROE

sugar cane fields. `Ewa had been a sugar plantation town since 1890. Some of the sugar delivered by the *Train de l'Amitié* came from `Ewa, and some people living in `Ewa were descended from those who'd grown and harvested the sugar cane and raised money for the *Friendship Train*. They just didn't know it. They, too, had forgotten.

The boxcar was taken to the Hawaiian Railway Society (HRS), an organization run by people in the Islands who love *nā ka`aahi* (trains or "fire wagons") and railroad history.

When it arrived, the HRS realized the boxcar needed help, but restoring boxcars is hard work and very expensive. It took a country to restore J-58220 in 1948, and Hawaiian Railway is a nonprofit group of volunteers. They didn't have the money or the manpower and they couldn't agree on what to do and how to do it. It was a very big project for a small organization. Some said the French boxcar wasn't a part of Hawai`i's history and should be scrapped. But others recognized its connection to Hawai`i's sugar heritage. One volunteer bought new shields and donated $4,000 to the renovation. People from *La Société des Quarante Hommes et Huit Chevaux* and "Merci Train" groups matched his donation and gave advice on how to restore the boxcar correctly. And while all of that was good, it wasn't enough. They needed more. A lot more.

Meanwhile other people came to visit the train yard and take pictures of the colorful locomotives and the big American boxcars. Sometimes they would glance at J-58220. Then they would walk away.

The years passed. The little French boxcar remained outside, exposed to the elements. The sun beat down, the rain fell, and the holes in the boxcar got bigger and bigger.

J-58220 was running out of time. Soon it would be too late.

Chapter 13

One day another man gazed very hard at the shabby, broken boxcar in the middle of the hot, dusty train yard. To most people, it was little more than rotten wood and rusty metal. But he was a veteran and a historian. He was very *akamai*. He recognized the "40 & 8" and knew why it was important to save it. He also knew if more people learned about the trains of *Friendship* and *Gratitude*, they would want to help save it, too.

The HRS still didn't have enough money or manpower for the entire project. They also didn't know exactly how much work J-58220 needed or the best way to get all that work done. The obstacles were overwhelming. But he knew they had enough money and willpower to begin.

He created an organized, detailed plan with step-by-step instructions and presented it to the HRS. He called it a "'living' document," to allow room for changes. It included the history of the *Friendship* and *Gratitude* trains and pictures of the boxcars filled with sugar from the people of Hawai`i. It also broke down the work into four categories: "mechanical, structural, wood siding/roof, and decoration."

The plan was approved and the volunteers got to work. Their first job was to install a new floor because what little wood remaining of the old floor was unsafe to stand on. Once they had a solid base, they focused their attention on preparing the rest of the boxcar for restoration. They removed more damaged wood, scraped off old paint, and sanded metal to get rid of the rust. They tried to save as many of the original parts as they could, but some things could not be reused. In that case, the plan recommended using original parts from 1949 or "suitable substitutes...following as closely as possible the original form fit and function."

The next step was to restore it. To do that, they needed more

paint, more wood, new roof beams, and the right kinds of metal parts. But they still didn't have enough money.

The akamai historian spread the word far and wide, reminding people of the true, heartwarming events ingrained with the spirit of kokua and aloha. At first, people didn't understand why an old boxcar from France was worth saving. But he explained why J-58220 was no ordinary boxcar and why it was important for us to remember this moment in history. As more and more people heard the unforgettable story, they were inspired and motivated by the actions of the French, the Americans, and the citizens of the Territory of Hawai`i long ago.

And the magic of *kokua* and *ka`aahi* happened a third time.

An organization that supports adults with disabilities heard the story and wanted to help. Their group of volunteers put a protective coat of primer on the frame above the floor.

Members of the Daughters of the American Revolution (DAR) came to the rail yard and organized DAR work days with their family and friends. For several days, they all volunteered their time painting things like the doors and the adornments to help make the boxcar look like a monument again.

Two men from the mainland, one from Pennsylvania and one from Tennessee, were also inspired by the story. They each spent part of their Hawaiian vacation busting rust and priming metal, instead of going to the beach like most tourists.

A member of the Architects and Engineers of Hawai`i volunteered his time and skills to work on the boxcar almost every Saturday for several months.

A veteran and the leader of a team that gets rid of unexploded ordnance (UXO) heard the story and wanted to help. His team of people, mostly veterans, offered to finish restoring the entire frame. They even crawled underneath the boxcar in the red dirt to prime and paint hard-to-reach areas.

Other people who couldn't do the physical work heard the unforgettable story and wanted to be a part of the restoration, so they donated money for supplies. One man wrote a check for $3,000 to cover the cost of a whole new roof. Twelve people gave $30 each to buy trusses, the special wood needed to support the roof. And people from "Merci Train" organizations were thrilled that the historic boxcar was getting the love it deserved, so they matched thousands of dollars in donations.

For twelve years the dedicated volunteers at Hawaiian Railway continued to work hard at bringing J-58220 back to life. They hammered, welded, and sawed. They made new friends and swapped stories. And as the history of the Friendship and Gratitude trains spread, people from all over came together and gave from their hearts in whatever way they could, all for the love of a little French boxcar.

Chapter 14

On February 2, 2025, members of the Hawaiian Railway Society, volunteers, guests from far and near, and television crews all gathered at the dry, dusty train yard to celebrate the "Merci" Boxcar 75th Anniversary Rededication Ceremony of Hawai`i's very own "40 & 8" and all the people who worked together to make this day a reality.

The ceremony began with a blessing in both English and Hawaiian. People bowed their heads respectfully as the minister uttered the words, *"E kō mākou Makua i loko o ka lani...."* (Our Father who art in heaven....) That was followed by many heartfelt speeches and a party. There were tables loaded with lots of food and a white cake decorated with a blue frosting lei. People enjoyed train rides and took pictures of the historic train cars, including the five colorful locomotives and the parlor car that Queen Lili`uokalani had ridden in.

But most of all, they gazed in awe at J-58220 standing proudly on a very special track made for a very special *kama`āina* boxcar. The holes and rotten wood were gone. It was painted a rich dark gray, and its metal frame was protected by a shiny new topcoat. It had new banners, new pictures of the eagle and steam engine, and new shields. It also had 40 *Hommes,* 8 *Chevaux* painted on its door again, which was important to those who had served.

The Hawaiian Railway Society continued to take very good care of J-58220, the newest member of their beloved historical `*ohana* (family). And people who loved trains and train rides came from far and near to visit it at its Hawaiian home. They took many pictures of it and gathered around the volunteers to hear the unforgettable true story of the little French boxcar that was built and delivered things over a century ago...

...and carried soldiers to battle and safety...
...and had a special group named after it...
...and helped a country regain its national pride...
...and brought gifts of gratitude across the ocean...
...to people who worked together to help people they never met...
...because like the ka`aahi steaming down the track, *kokua, amitié,* and *merci* run on *aloha.*

"...I feel the need to tell you what the French people want to express to your great country by this symbolic train.
To you Americans who have done so much, given so much to our children, the aged, and the people of France, it is an affectionate thanks, the sincere gratitude of my country. This train, made of cars that your GI's know well, is a token of our affection, of our friendship to all of your 48 states. Each one of these cars...will tell those of you who know us, that we do not forget. And to those of you who never come to our land, may it bring a message from the people of France to all the people of the U.S.A. In dawn of 1949, I see this gesture of friendship more than an omen, more than a message, I see in it a pledge that men can love and understand each other when they silence their self interest and only listen to their hearts."

-Letter from Louis Brenel, a paralyzed French veteran, writing from a hospital in Paris.

HOMMES 40
GRATITUDE TRAIN
P.L.M
J 5822

PRONUNCIATION GUIDE

How to say the Hawaiian, Japanese, and French words used in this story:

Hawaiian

'Āina – EYE-nuh

Akamai – ah-kuh-MY

'Aloha' – aaa-LOW-hah

'Ewa – EH-vuh

Hawai'i – hah-VEYE-ee

Honouliuli – hah-no-oo-LEE-oo-lee

Ka`aahi – KAH-ah-ah-hee

Kama'āina – ka-mah-EYE-nuh

Kamehameha – KAH-may-ha-may-ha

Kānaka – kuh-NAW-kuh

Kānaka Maoli – Kuh-NAW-kuh MAH-oh-lee

Keiki – KAY-kee

Kokua – ko-KOO-uh

Lili`uokalani – LIL-ee-oo-oh-kah-LAH-nee

Laulima – lau-LEE-muh

Malihini – mah-LEE-hee-nee

'Ōlelo Hawai`i – o-LEH-lo hah-VEYE-ee

O`ahu – o-AH-hu

`Ohana – O-HA-nuh

Pu'uloa – poo-OO-low-ah

Japanese

Issei – eee-say

Nisei – nee-say

French

Aisne-Marne – EHN-marn

Fleur-des-lis – flur-duh-LEE

La Société des Quarante Hommes et Huit Chevaux – la soh-see-ay-tay day kah-rahnt ohm ay weet sh-voo

Le Havre – luh-AHV-ruh

Lyon – Lee-YAWN

Musée du Louvre – moo-ZAY doo LOO-vruh

Marseille – mar-SAY

Merci – mehr-SEE

Montparnasse – mohn-par-NASS

Saint-Dié-des-Vosges – san-dyay-day-VOZH

Sévres – SEV-ruh

Symboles de France – sim-bohl duh FRAHNS

Train de l'Amitié – tran duh lah-mee-TAY

Train de la Reconnaissance Francaise – tran duh lah ruh-koh-nay-SAHNS frahn-SEZ

Vive la France – veev la FRAHNS

Thank you for reading The Unforgettable Boxcar! If you would like to learn more about this fascinating moment in history, visit the Merci Train - Home Page (www.mercitrain.org).

If you would like to see pictures of J-58220 or learn more about our journey bringing this book to life, visit www.theunforgettableboxcar.com or scan the QR code below:

ACKNOWLEDGEMENTS

This book couldn't have been written without the *kokua,* help, support and encouragement from so many kind and wonderful people from all over the world. From the bottom of our grateful hearts, we say merci, mahalo, we love you all and thank you to:

Ellen Wettersten, our eagle-eyed editor. From the very beginning she took our manuscript and elevated it to the next level after we were convinced that it was the cleanest manuscript ever. Possessing a keen eye for details, she even spotted an error we made with a word in Hawaiian! Most of all, she fell in love with the events of 1947 through 1949 and beyond just as much as we had. She was a joy to work with. Ellen can be found at www.Reedsy.com.

Claudia Gadotti, our incredible illustrator who truly deserves the title award-winning. Her amazing portfolio speaks for itself. We were beyond thrilled when she agreed to work with us. She brought the events of our story to life in such rich detail, and did so with incredible patience. Even after the insane number of historical photographs we sent, she mercilessly did not give up on two crazy authors. You can find Claudia on www.Reedsy.com.

Jane Sweetland, author of the meticulously researched *Boxcar Diplomacy: Two Trains That Crossed an Ocean,* the very best book you can own to understand the events of 1947 through 1949. Jane was generous and gracious enough to not only provide historical information, but also to cheer us on. We each have a treasured copy of her book, and our copies are well-thumbed, dog-eared, highlighted and bristling with post-it notes. If you want to know more about the amazing story of the Friendship Train, the Gratitude Train, and the Merci boxcars (and there is more), read her book.

Jeff Livingston, the Hawaiian Railway Society's Historian and the man who spearheaded the restoration of Hawaii's Merci boxcar. Thank you so much for patiently answering our questions (read: replying to the countless flow of emails in a timely manner without pulling the plug on us), checking the accuracy of our manuscript and sending us real time updates on the restoration. We are lucky to have someone so *akamai* in our corner!

Alexis Muller, a man of infinite knowledge regarding the history of the Merci Boxcars as well as the rich history and culture of France from a French perspective. Alexis helped us understand why the Merci Boxcars were monuments to the incredible bond forged between the veterans of France and America through two world wars. Once he accomplished that while making breakfast for his family. You can find Alexis multitasking for the Merci Train Organization on Facebook.

Kevin Yamamoto, the Hawaiian Railway Society's Director of Restoration. Kevin took over a hundred photos of the train yard at Ewa to serve as our "eyes" in order to set the scene for the book's illustrations (and also made us anxious to visit home again). *Mahalo*, Kevin, for taking the time out of your busy schedule!

Marnie Butu is a wonderful, caring person and the most dedicated children's librarian on the planet. We turned to Marnie for advice about picture books, readability, non-fiction books for younger and older readers, and illustrations, both photo and drawn. We appreciate all the little details you helped us with, as well as the book samples you sent (gold mine!) Thank you so much for taking time out of your busy work and life schedule to help us! We couldn't have done this without you!

John and Sue Ann Irving, members of both the Hawaiian Railway Society and the Merci Train Organization, who gently pushed for the restoration of the boxcar. John and Sue Ann did everything from being another set of eyes on the manuscript, to answering myriad questions, as well as connecting us to people and websites that could help even more.

The Merci Train Organization: This group of dedicated Merci Train lovers is keeping an important page of history alive. They gave us permission to use the official Merci Train logo, and although no one seems to quite know who to credit for this beautiful drawing, we say thank you, *mahalo,* and *merci.*

The Hawaiian Railway Society: Formed in 1970, HRS has dedicated more than 50 years to keeping the history of railroading in Hawaii alive. They give narrated train rides, restore historic railroad equipment, and maintain 15 miles of historic track. Best of all, they took in the Merci boxcar when it had nowhere else to go.

The Librarians and Staff at the Los Angeles Public Library Mar Vista branch: A very big *mahalo* for all the recommendations and published examples of really good children's and middle-grade historical non-fiction books. You not only opened up a world for us but you didn't bat an eye when we said we were writing one. And you cheered us on! Even when we said we'd never written one before! In a town where it seems like everyone is either a writer or an actor (or is six degrees from one) that enthusiasm is unprecedented. Seriously, librarians are superheroes. Take good care of them, you never know when you'll need one (or a team).

Our Beta Readers: These wonderful advocates served as a second set of eyes, reading the manuscript to give us important feedback before we turned it over to Ellen. We appreciate your time and feedback to help make *The Unforgettable Boxcar* a better book. They include:

Jeff Livingston

John & Sue Ann Irving

Marnie Butu

Mirella Butu

Lori Arizumi

Agnes Laurent

Alexandra Durazzano

Our Translators: These kind and generous people not only tackled our pronunciation guide to help us and our readers sound out words in Hawaiian, Japanese, and French, but they also educated us on the proper way some of these words are meant to be used in a bilingual sentence. The honor of working with you was a lovely reminder of how we are all connected:

Lori Arizumi

Elarka Yuen

Agnes Laurent

Kau`i Norton

Alexis Muller

Mahalo Nui Loa!
(thank you very much)

ABOUT THE AUTHORS

Janet Lorimer: Janet has been writing professionally for over 40 years. Her first sale was a story made to *Highlights for Children* magazine in 1981. She subsequently published a picture book, *The Biggest Bubble* in the World, with Franklin Watts in 1982, and three children's novels, *The Mystery of the Missing Treasure* (1987), *The Mystery of the Haunted Trail* (1989), and *The Trouble with Buster* (1990), with Scholastic, Inc. She also published over 60 high interest/low reading level books used in literacy and English-As-A-Second-Language classes.
Thirty years ago, she was appointed the editor for the Hawaiian Railway Society's newsletter, *Akahele I Ke Ka`aahi*, and she's been producing it ever since. It continues to be one of her favorite things to do.

Kerry Lorimer: After a summer driving Disneyland's Monorail, Kerry worked at the Hawaiian Railway Society as a narrator and flagman, leaping off moving trains between spiels and racing into intersections to stop the flow of traffic so the train could cross. Nine lives later, she became hooked on writing when her first article was published in the magazine for the American Judo and Jujitsu Federation, *Kiai Echo*. A proud member of The Alliance of Independent Authors (ALLi), she also writes about snarky vampires under the pseudonym Scarlet Kay. *The Unforgettable Boxcar* is her first middle-grade book.

BIBLIOGRAPHY

BOOKS

Sweetland, Jane. *Boxcar Diplomacy: Two Trains That Crossed an Ocean.* 2019. ISBN 979-8-218-17965-6

ARTICLES

The Honolulu Star-Bulletin, "Friendship Train May Get Carload of Hawaii Sugar," October 31, 1947

The Honolulu Star-Bulletin, "Drive for Funds in High Gear; Headquarters Open," November 1, 1947

The Honolulu Star-Bulletin, "Hawaii Responding Generously to 'Friendship Train' Drive," November 3, 1947

The Honolulu Star-Bulletin, "Delegate Praises Hawaii's 'Friendship Train' Offering," November 4, 1947

The Honolulu Star-Bulletin, "Hanahauoli School 'Friendship Train' Draws Net $16.60," "Sugar Arithmetic," "Kailua Students Asking Donations," November 5, 1947

The Honolulu Star-Bulletin, "$5,000 Already Collected," November 6, 1947

The Honolulu Star-Bulletin, "Hawaii's Sugar Joins the 'Friendship Train' Today," "Hawaii in Limelight at Hollywood Friendship Train Ceremonies," "Hawaii's Friendship Gift Is Being Given National Publicity," November 8, 1947

The Honolulu Star-Bulletin, "Governor to Report on Friendship Train Sendoff," "Teamwork of Friendship Train Noted," November 10, 1947

Pearson, Drew, "Friendship Train Piled High; Hawaii's Contribution Is Cited," Washington Merry-Go-Round, The Honolulu Star-Bulletin, November 11, 1947

The Honolulu Star-Bulletin, "Merci Train," January 12, 1949, Page 26

The Honolulu Advertiser, "'Merci' Gifts Go To Oahu Easter Babies," April 19, 1949, Page 1

Oshiro, Dorothy, "Farrington Student Wins Contest in French," The Honolulu Advertiser, June 4, 1950, Page 7

The Honolulu Star-Bulletin, "French Box Car Serves Legion," May 24, 1952, Page 9

Nelson, Lyle, "Boxcar without a home," The Honolulu Star-Bulletin, February 23, 1966, Page 6

ARTICLES WITH WEBSITES

Ciarelli, P., The French Merci Boxcar, October 6, 2021, https://sewivets.org/Voiture410/the-french-merci-boxcar/

Patowary, Ava, The Merci Train: 49 Boxcars Filled with Gratitude, May 12, 2016, https://www.amusingplanet.com/2016/05/the-merci-train-49-boxcars-filled-with.html

Scheele, Dorothy, "The Friendship Train of 1947," https://thefriendshiptrain1947.org/

Wilkey, Ava, The Forty and Eight Merci Boxcar: A Gift to our Greatest Generation, http://mercitrain.org/Georgia/merci_car_wilkey20070409.pdf

Go For Broke National Education Center, https://goforbroke.org/history/unit-history/442nd-regimental-combat-team/

French Gratitude Train, State Historical Society of North Dakota, https://www.history.nd.gov/fgt/index.html

Friendship Train to France, Ames History Museum, https://ameshistory.org/content/friendship-train-france

French Merci Boxcar – 40 et 8 The French Merci Boxcar – 40 et 8 Voiture 410 Kenosha County, WI, https://sewivets.org/Voiture410/

From Friendship to Gratitude - The Merci Train Collection | Arizona Memory Project
https://azmemory.azlibrary.gov/nodes/view/231

"History and Culture: Honouliuli Internment Camp," National Park Service, Honouliuli National Historic Site, Hawaii, https://www.nps.gov/hono/learn/historyculture/index.htm

The Railroad Press, "The Merci Train 1949," October-November-December 1999, https://utahrails.net/utahrails/merci-train.htm

"September 1, 1946: Hawaiian Sugar Plantation Workers Stage Mass Strike," https://www.zinnedproject.org/news/tdih/hawaiian-sugar-plantation-strike/

"1946 The Great Hawai`i Sugar Strike, Rice and Roses," https://www.hawaii.edu/uhwo/clear/home/1946.html

The 1949 French Merci Train / Gratitude Train / Train De Le Reconnaissance Francaise
https://www.themtrains.com/merci-train-main.html

https://sewivets.org/Voiture410/wp-content/uploads/2021/10/The-French-Merci-Boxcar-Story.pdf

Merci Train Facts for Kids, https://kids.kiddle.co/Merci_Train

Wikipedia, https://en.wikipedia.org/wiki/friendship_train

Wikipedia, https://en.wikipedia.org/wiki/Merci_Train

Wikipedia, https://en.wikipedia.org/wiki/Hawaiian_sugar_strike_of_1946

RESOURCES

Forty and Eights (www.fortyandeight.org)
442nd Regimental Combat Team Legacy (the442.org)
Merci Train Organization (www.mercitrain.org)
The Hawaiian Railway Society (www.hawaiianrailway.com)
Livingston, Jeff, "Restoration Plan for French Boxcar PLM #J-58220," Original 12 May 2022

On YouTube in the Search Window, you can type in any of the key words (Friendship Train, Gratitude Train, Merci boxcars) and you will discover videos of the actual trains and boxcars.

www.ingramcontent.com/pod-product-compliance
Lightning Source LLC
La Vergne TN
LVHW090908151225
827608LV00002B/26
* 9 7 9 8 9 9 9 0 7 1 1 2 5 *